MY PE

AXOLOTL LOGBOOK

THIS BOOK BELONGS TO:

MY PET
AXOLOTL LOGBOOK

ALL ABOUT YOUR AXOLOTL

PHOTO/DRAWING

NICKNAME:

DOB:

SPECIES:

SEX:

COLOR & MARKING:

LINCENSE #:

ADOPTION PLACE:

MORPH:

MICROCHIP:

HOW WE MET:

HOW HE/HER GOT NAME:

OWNER'S INFORMATION

NAME:

ADDRESS:

PHONE: EMAIL:

VET INFORMATION

CLINIC: VET:

ADDRESS:

PHONE: EMAIL:

IMPORTANT NUMBERS

NAME:	PHONE:	ADDRESS:

NOTES:

SUPPLIES CHECKLIST

- ☐ 2ft tank or larger
- ☐ Fine sand
- ☐ Filter
- ☐ Driftwood
- ☐ Plants
- ☐ Water conditioner
- ☐ Bio culture
- ☐ Net
- ☐ pH test kit
- ☐ Amonia test kit
- ☐ Nitrite test kit
- ☐ Nitrate test kit
- ☐ Axolotl pellets
- ☐ Frozen food
- ☐ Crickets
- ☐ Worms

# MEDICATION RECORD/VET VISITS

DATE:	REASON FOR VISIT:	NEXT VISIT:
DATE:	REASON FOR VISIT:	NEXT VISIT:
DATE:	REASON FOR VISIT:	NEXT VISIT:
DATE:	REASON FOR VISIT:	NEXT VISIT:
DATE:	REASON FOR VISIT:	NEXT VISIT:
DATE:	REASON FOR VISIT:	NEXT VISIT:
DATE:	REASON FOR VISIT:	NEXT VISIT:

EXPENSES

DATE:	SOURCE	DESCRIPTION:	AMOUNT:

DATE: AGE:

OBSERVATIONS:

DATE: AGE:

OBSERVATIONS:

DATE: AGE:

OBSERVATIONS:

DATE: AGE:

OBSERVATIONS:

DATE: AGE:

OBSERVATIONS:

DATE: AGE:

OBSERVATIONS:

DATE: AGE:

OBSERVATIONS:

DATE: AGE:

OBSERVATIONS:

12 MONTH AROWANA PROGRESS JOURNAL

DATE: AGE:

OBSERVATIONS:

DATE: AGE:

OBSERVATIONS:

DATE: AGE:

OBSERVATIONS:

DATE: AGE:

OBSERVATIONS:

ABOUT AXOLOTL

life span
- 10 to 15 years

Size
- Adult Size 6 to 18 inches in length 5 to 12 ounces

Diet
- Carnivore

Temperature:
- 60-70°F (15-23°C)

PH
- 6.5-8.0

DAILY CHECKLIST

Activity	WEEK OF						
	SUN	MON	TUE	WED	THU	FRI	SAT
Feed axolotl 2-3 x week	☑	☑	☑	☑	☑	☐	☑
Remove uneaten food	☑	☐	☑	☑	☑	☑	☑
Check filter	☐	☐	☐	☐	☐	☐	☐
Check water temperature	☑	☑	☑	☑	☑	☑	☑
Check other equipment	☐	☐	☐	☐	☐	☐	☐
Visual Inspect	☑	☑	☑	☑	☑	☐	☑
	☐	☐	☐	☐	☐	☐	☐

NOTES:

WEEKLY, MONTHLY CHECKLIST

WEEKLY ACTIVITY   DATE:

- [ ] Test check water quality
- [ ] Change water 20% of the water each week
- [✓] Vacuum up uneaten food and waste
- [ ] Check pH and bacteria levels
- [ ] Healthy checklist

MONTHLY ACTIVITY MONTH:

- [ ] Check filters, replacing media as necessary
- [ ] Clean fake plants, decorations, & algae
- [✓] Vacuum up all waste & uneaten food from gravel
- [ ] Check water quality & pH levels

HEALTH CHECKLIST   DATE: 25/11/23

- [✓] [ ] Fluffy gills
- [✓] [ ] Round belly (same size as head)
- [✓] [ ] Gills back
- [✓] [ ] No skin damage
- [✓] [✓] Active (for an axolotl)

NOTES: unusually
active (for an axolotl)

HIGHLIGHT OF THE WEEK:

DAILY CHECKLIST

Activity	WEEK OF	SUN	MON	TUE	WED	THU	FRI	SAT
Feed axolotl 2-3 x week		☐	☐	☐	☐	☐	☐	☐
Remove uneaten food		☐	☐	☐	☐	☐	☐	☐
Check filter		☐	☐	☐	☐	☐	☐	☐
Check water temperature		☐	☐	☐	☐	☐	☐	☐
Check other equipment		☐	☐	☐	☐	☐	☐	☐
Visual Inspect		☐	☐	☐	☐	☐	☐	☐
		☐	☐	☐	☐	☐	☐	☐

NOTES:

WEEKLY, MONTHLY CHECKLIST

WEEKLY ACTIVITY   DATE: [   ]

- [ ] Test check water quality
- [ ] Change water 20% of the water each week
- [ ] Vacuum up uneaten food and waste
- [ ] Check pH and bacteria levels
- [ ] Healthy checklist

MONTHLY ACTIVITY MONTH: [   ]

- [ ] Check filters, replacing media as necessary
- [ ] Clean fake plants, decorations, & algae
- [ ] Vacuum up all waste & uneaten food from gravel
- [ ] Check water quality & pH levels

HEALTH CHECKLIST   DATE: [   ]

- [Y] [N] Fluffy gills
- [Y] [N] Round belly (same size as head)
- [Y] [N] Gills back
- [Y] [N] No skin damage
- [Y] [N] Active (for an axolotl)

NOTES:

HIGHLIGHT OF THE WEEK:

DAILY CHECKLIST

Activity	SUN	MON	TUE	WED	THU	FRI	SAT
WEEK OF _____							
Feed axolotl 2-3 x week	☐	☐	☐	☐	☐	☐	☐
Remove uneaten food	☐	☐	☐	☐	☐	☐	☐
Check filter	☐	☐	☐	☐	☐	☐	☐
Check water temperature	☐	☐	☐	☐	☐	☐	☐
Check other equipment	☐	☐	☐	☐	☐	☐	☐
Visual Inspect	☐	☐	☐	☐	☐	☐	☐
	☐	☐	☐	☐	☐	☐	☐

NOTES:

WEEKLY, MONTHLY CHECKLIST

WEEKLY ACTIVITY   DATE: [   ]

- [ ] Test check water quality
- [ ] Change water 20% of the water each week
- [ ] Vacuum up uneaten food and waste
- [ ] Check pH and bacteria levels
- [ ] Healthy checklist

MONTHLY ACTIVITY   MONTH: [   ]

- [ ] Check filters, replacing media as necessary
- [ ] Clean fake plants, decorations, & algae
- [ ] Vacuum up all waste & uneaten food from gravel
- [ ] Check water quality & pH levels

HEALTH CHECKLIST   DATE: [   ]

- [ ] [ ] Fluffy gills
- [ ] [ ] Round belly (same size as head)
- [ ] [ ] Gills back
- [ ] [ ] No skin damage
- [ ] [ ] Active (for an axolotl)

NOTES:

HIGHLIGHT OF THE WEEK:

DAILY CHECKLIST

Activity	SUN	MON	TUE	WED	THU	FRI	SAT
WEEK OF							
Feed axolotl 2-3 x week	☐	☐	☐	☐	☐	☐	☐
Remove uneaten food	☐	☐	☐	☐	☐	☐	☐
Check filter	☐	☐	☐	☐	☐	☐	☐
Check water temperature	☐	☐	☐	☐	☐	☐	☐
Check other equipment	☐	☐	☐	☐	☐	☐	☐
Visual Inspect	☐	☐	☐	☐	☐	☐	☐
	☐	☐	☐	☐	☐	☐	☐

NOTES:

WEEKLY, MONTHLY CHECKLIST

WEEKLY ACTIVITY   DATE: [   ]

- [ ] Test check water quality
- [ ] Change water 20% of the water each week
- [ ] Vacuum up uneaten food and waste
- [ ] Check pH and bacteria levels
- [ ] Healthy checklist

MONTHLY ACTIVITY   MONTH: [   ]

- [ ] Check filters, replacing media as necessary
- [ ] Clean fake plants, decorations, & algae
- [ ] Vacuum up all waste & uneaten food from gravel
- [ ] Check water quality & pH levels

HEALTH CHECKLIST   DATE: [   ]

- [ ] [ ] Fluffy gills
- [ ] [ ] Round belly (same size as head)
- [ ] [ ] Gills back
- [ ] [ ] No skin damage
- [ ] [ ] Active (for an axolotl)

NOTES:

HIGHLIGHT OF THE WEEK:

DAILY CHECKLIST

Activity	WEEK OF						
	SUN	MON	TUE	WED	THU	FRI	SAT
Feed axolotl 2-3 x week	☐	☐	☐	☐	☐	☐	☐
Remove uneaten food	☐	☐	☐	☐	☐	☐	☐
Check filter	☐	☐	☐	☐	☐	☐	☐
Check water temperature	☐	☐	☐	☐	☐	☐	☐
Check other equipment	☐	☐	☐	☐	☐	☐	☐
Visual Inspect	☐	☐	☐	☐	☐	☐	☐
	☐	☐	☐	☐	☐	☐	☐

NOTES:

WEEKLY, MONTHLY CHECKLIST

WEEKLY ACTIVITY   DATE: [   ]

- [ ] Test check water quality
- [ ] Change water 20% of the water each week
- [ ] Vacuum up uneaten food and waste
- [ ] Check pH and bacteria levels
- [ ] Healthy checklist

MONTHLY ACTIVITY   MONTH: [   ]

- [ ] Check filters, replacing media as necessary
- [ ] Clean fake plants, decorations, & algae
- [ ] Vacuum up all waste & uneaten food from gravel
- [ ] Check water quality & pH levels

HEALTH CHECKLIST   DATE: [   ]

- [Y] [N] Fluffy gills
- [Y] [N] Round belly (same size as head)
- [Y] [N] Gills back
- [ ] [ ] No skin damage
- [Y] [N] Active (for an axolotl)

NOTES:

HIGHLIGHT OF THE WEEK:

DAILY CHECKLIST

Activity	WEEK OF						
	SUN	MON	TUE	WED	THU	FRI	SAT
Feed axolotl 2-3 x week	☐	☐	☐	☐	☐	☐	☐
Remove uneaten food	☐	☐	☐	☐	☐	☐	☐
Check filter	☐	☐	☐	☐	☐	☐	☐
Check water temperature	☐	☐	☐	☐	☐	☐	☐
Check other equipment	☐	☐	☐	☐	☐	☐	☐
Visual Inspect	☐	☐	☐	☐	☐	☐	☐
	☐	☐	☐	☐	☐	☐	☐

NOTES:

WEEKLY, MONTHLY CHECKLIST

WEEKLY ACTIVITY   DATE: [____]

- [ ] Test check water quality
- [ ] Change water 20% of the water each week
- [ ] Vacuum up uneaten food and waste
- [ ] Check pH and bacteria levels
- [ ] Healthy checklist

MONTHLY ACTIVITY   MONTH: [____]

- [ ] Check filters, replacing media as necessary
- [ ] Clean fake plants, decorations, & algae
- [ ] Vacuum up all waste & uneaten food from gravel
- [ ] Check water quality & pH levels

HEALTH CHECKLIST   DATE: [____]

- [ ] [ ] Fluffy gills
- [ ] [ ] Round belly (same size as head)
- [ ] [ ] Gills back
- [ ] [ ] No skin damage
- [ ] [ ] Active (for an axolotl)

NOTES:

HIGHLIGHT OF THE WEEK:

DAILY CHECKLIST

Activity	WEEK OF						
	SUN	MON	TUE	WED	THU	FRI	SAT
Feed axolotl 2-3 x week	☐	☐	☐	☐	☐	☐	☐
Remove uneaten food	☐	☐	☐	☐	☐	☐	☐
Check filter	☐	☐	☐	☐	☐	☐	☐
Check water temperature	☐	☐	☐	☐	☐	☐	☐
Check other equipment	☐	☐	☐	☐	☐	☐	☐
Visual Inspect	☐	☐	☐	☐	☐	☐	☐
	☐	☐	☐	☐	☐	☐	☐

NOTES:

WEEKLY, MONTHLY CHECKLIST

WEEKLY ACTIVITY   DATE: ☐

- ☐ Test check water quality
- ☐ Change water 20% of the water each week
- ☐ Vacuum up uneaten food and waste
- ☐ Check pH and bacteria levels
- ☐ Healthy checklist

MONTHLY ACTIVITY   MONTH: ☐

- ☐ Check filters, replacing media as necessary
- ☐ Clean fake plants, decorations, & algae
- ☐ Vacuum up all waste & uneaten food from gravel
- ☐ Check water quality & pH levels

HEALTH CHECKLIST   DATE: ☐

- ☐ ☐ Fluffy gills
- ☐ ☐ Round belly (same size as head)
- ☐ ☐ Gills back
- ☐ ☐ No skin damage
- ☐ ☐ Active (for an axolotl)

NOTES:

HIGHLIGHT OF THE WEEK:

DAILY CHECKLIST

Activity	 WEEK OF						
	SUN	MON	TUE	WED	THU	FRI	SAT
Feed axolotl 2-3 x week	☐	☐	☐	☐	☐	☐	☐
Remove uneaten food	☐	☐	☐	☐	☐	☐	☐
Check filter	☐	☐	☐	☐	☐	☐	☐
Check water temperature	☐	☐	☐	☐	☐	☐	☐
Check other equipment	☐	☐	☐	☐	☐	☐	☐
Visual Inspect	☐	☐	☐	☐	☐	☐	☐
	☐	☐	☐	☐	☐	☐	☐

NOTES:

WEEKLY, MONTHLY CHECKLIST

WEEKLY ACTIVITY   DATE: [____]

- [ ] Test check water quality
- [ ] Change water 20% of the water each week
- [ ] Vacuum up uneaten food and waste
- [ ] Check pH and bacteria levels
- [ ] Healthy checklist

MONTHLY ACTIVITY   MONTH: [____]

- [ ] Check filters, replacing media as necessary
- [ ] Clean fake plants, decorations, & algae
- [ ] Vacuum up all waste & uneaten food from gravel
- [ ] Check water quality & pH levels

HEALTH CHECKLIST   DATE: [____]

- [ ] [Y] [ ] [N] Fluffy gills
- [ ] [Y] [ ] [N] Round belly (same size as head)
- [ ] [Y] [ ] [N] Gills back
- [ ] [Y] [ ] [N] No skin damage
- [ ] [Y] [ ] [N] Active (for an axolotl)

NOTES:

HIGHLIGHT OF THE WEEK:

DAILY CHECKLIST

Activity	WEEK OF						
	SUN	MON	TUE	WED	THU	FRI	SAT
Feed axolotl 2-3 x week	☐	☐	☐	☐	☐	☐	☐
Remove uneaten food	☐	☐	☐	☐	☐	☐	☐
Check filter	☐	☐	☐	☐	☐	☐	☐
Check water temperature	☐	☐	☐	☐	☐	☐	☐
Check other equipment	☐	☐	☐	☐	☐	☐	☐
Visual Inspect	☐	☐	☐	☐	☐	☐	☐
	☐	☐	☐	☐	☐	☐	☐

NOTES:

WEEKLY, MONTHLY CHECKLIST

WEEKLY ACTIVITY   DATE: [   ]

- [ ] Test check water quality
- [ ] Change water 20% of the water each week
- [ ] Vacuum up uneaten food and waste
- [ ] Check pH and bacteria levels
- [ ] Healthy checklist

MONTHLY ACTIVITY   MONTH: [   ]

- [ ] Check filters, replacing media as necessary
- [ ] Clean fake plants, decorations, & algae
- [ ] Vacuum up all waste & uneaten food from gravel
- [ ] Check water quality & pH levels

HEALTH CHECKLIST   DATE: [   ]

- [ ] [ ] Fluffy gills
- [ ] [ ] Round belly (same size as head)
- [ ] [ ] Gills back
- [ ] [ ] No skin damage
- [ ] [ ] Active (for an axolotl)

NOTES:

HIGHLIGHT OF THE WEEK:

DAILY CHECKLIST

Activity	WEEK OF						
	SUN	MON	TUE	WED	THU	FRI	SAT
Feed axolotl 2-3 x week	☐	☐	☐	☐	☐	☐	☐
Remove uneaten food	☐	☐	☐	☐	☐	☐	☐
Check filter	☐	☐	☐	☐	☐	☐	☐
Check water temperature	☐	☐	☐	☐	☐	☐	☐
Check other equipment	☐	☐	☐	☐	☐	☐	☐
Visual Inspect	☐	☐	☐	☐	☐	☐	☐
	☐	☐	☐	☐	☐	☐	☐

NOTES:

WEEKLY, MONTHLY CHECKLIST

WEEKLY ACTIVITY   DATE: [   ]

- [ ] Test check water quality
- [ ] Change water 20% of the water each week
- [ ] Vacuum up uneaten food and waste
- [ ] Check pH and bacteria levels
- [ ] Healthy checklist

MONTHLY ACTIVITY   MONTH: [   ]

- [ ] Check filters, replacing media as necessary
- [ ] Clean fake plants, decorations, & algae
- [ ] Vacuum up all waste & uneaten food from gravel
- [ ] Check water quality & pH levels

HEALTH CHECKLIST   DATE: [   ]

- [ ] [ ] Fluffy gills
- [ ] [ ] Round belly (same size as head)
- [ ] [ ] Gills back
- [ ] [ ] No skin damage
- [ ] [ ] Active (for an axolotl)

NOTES:

HIGHLIGHT OF THE WEEK:

DAILY CHECKLIST

Activity	WEEK OF						
	SUN	MON	TUE	WED	THU	FRI	SAT
Feed axolotl 2-3 x week	☐	☐	☐	☐	☐	☐	☐
Remove uneaten food	☐	☐	☐	☐	☐	☐	☐
Check filter	☐	☐	☐	☐	☐	☐	☐
Check water temperature	☐	☐	☐	☐	☐	☐	☐
Check other equipment	☐	☐	☐	☐	☐	☐	☐
Visual Inspect	☐	☐	☐	☐	☐	☐	☐
	☐	☐	☐	☐	☐	☐	☐

NOTES:

WEEKLY, MONTHLY CHECKLIST

WEEKLY ACTIVITY   DATE: [ ]

- [ ] Test check water quality
- [ ] Change water 20% of the water each week
- [ ] Vacuum up uneaten food and waste
- [ ] Check pH and bacteria levels
- [ ] Healthy checklist

MONTHLY ACTIVITY   MONTH: [ ]

- [ ] Check filters, replacing media as necessary
- [ ] Clean fake plants, decorations, & algae
- [ ] Vacuum up all waste & uneaten food from gravel
- [ ] Check water quality & pH levels

HEALTH CHECKLIST   DATE: [ ]

- [Y] [N] Fluffy gills
- [Y] [N] Round belly (same size as head)
- [Y] [N] Gills back
- [Y] [N] No skin damage
- [Y] [N] Active (for an axolotl)

NOTES:

HIGHLIGHT OF THE WEEK:

DAILY CHECKLIST

Activity	WEEK OF						
	SUN	MON	TUE	WED	THU	FRI	SAT
Feed axolotl 2-3 x week	☐	☐	☐	☐	☐	☐	☐
Remove uneaten food	☐	☐	☐	☐	☐	☐	☐
Check filter	☐	☐	☐	☐	☐	☐	☐
Check water temperature	☐	☐	☐	☐	☐	☐	☐
Check other equipment	☐	☐	☐	☐	☐	☐	☐
Visual Inspect	☐	☐	☐	☐	☐	☐	☐
	☐	☐	☐	☐	☐	☐	☐

NOTES:

WEEKLY, MONTHLY CHECKLIST

WEEKLY ACTIVITY   DATE: [____]

- ☐ Test check water quality
- ☐ Change water 20% of the water each week
- ☐ Vacuum up uneaten food and waste
- ☐ Check pH and bacteria levels
- ☐ Healthy checklist

MONTHLY ACTIVITY MONTH: [____]

- ☐ Check filters, replacing media as necessary
- ☐ Clean fake plants, decorations, & algae
- ☐ Vacuum up all waste & uneaten food from gravel
- ☐ Check water quality & pH levels

HEALTH CHECKLIST   DATE: [____]

- ☐Y ☐N Fluffy gills
- ☐Y ☐N Round belly (same size as head)
- ☐Y ☐N Gills back
- ☐Y ☐N No skin damage
- ☐Y ☐N Active (for an axolotl)

NOTES:

HIGHLIGHT OF THE WEEK:

DAILY CHECKLIST

Activity	WEEK OF						
	SUN	MON	TUE	WED	THU	FRI	SAT
Feed axolotl 2-3 x week	☐	☐	☐	☐	☐	☐	☐
Remove uneaten food	☐	☐	☐	☐	☐	☐	☐
Check filter	☐	☐	☐	☐	☐	☐	☐
Check water temperature	☐	☐	☐	☐	☐	☐	☐
Check other equipment	☐	☐	☐	☐	☐	☐	☐
Visual Inspect	☐	☐	☐	☐	☐	☐	☐
	☐	☐	☐	☐	☐	☐	☐

NOTES:

WEEKLY, MONTHLY CHECKLIST

- [ ] Test check water quality
- [ ] Change water 20% of the water each week
- [ ] Vacuum up uneaten food and waste
- [ ] Check pH and bacteria levels
- [ ] Healthy checklist

MONTHLY ACTIVITY   MONTH: [   ]

- [ ] Check filters, replacing media as necessary
- [ ] Clean fake plants, decorations, & algae
- [ ] Vacuum up all waste & uneaten food from gravel
- [ ] Check water quality & pH levels

HEALTH CHECKLIST   DATE: [   ]

- [Y] [N] Fluffy gills
- [Y] [N] Round belly (same size as head)
- [Y] [N] Gills back
- [ ] [ ] No skin damage
- [Y] [N] Active (for an axolotl)

NOTES:

HIGHLIGHT OF THE WEEK:

DAILY CHECKLIST

Activity	WEEK OF

	SUN	MON	TUE	WED	THU	FRI	SAT
Feed axolotl 2-3 x week	☐	☐	☐	☐	☐	☐	☐
Remove uneaten food	☐	☐	☐	☐	☐	☐	☐
Check filter	☐	☐	☐	☐	☐	☐	☐
Check water temperature	☐	☐	☐	☐	☐	☐	☐
Check other equipment	☐	☐	☐	☐	☐	☐	☐
Visual Inspect	☐	☐	☐	☐	☐	☐	☐
	☐	☐	☐	☐	☐	☐	☐

NOTES:

WEEKLY, MONTHLY CHECKLIST

WEEKLY ACTIVITY   DATE: _____

- [ ] Test check water quality
- [ ] Change water 20% of the water each week
- [ ] Vacuum up uneaten food and waste
- [ ] Check pH and bacteria levels
- [ ] Healthy checklist

MONTHLY ACTIVITY   MONTH: _____

- [ ] Check filters, replacing media as necessary
- [ ] Clean fake plants, decorations, & algae
- [ ] Vacuum up all waste & uneaten food from gravel
- [ ] Check water quality & pH levels

HEALTH CHECKLIST   DATE: _____

- [Y] [N] Fluffy gills
- [Y] [N] Round belly (same size as head)
- [Y] [N] Gills back
- [Y] [N] No skin damage
- [Y] [N] Active (for an axolotl)

NOTES:

HIGHLIGHT OF THE WEEK:

DAILY CHECKLIST

Activity	WEEK OF						
	SUN	MON	TUE	WED	THU	FRI	SAT
Feed axolotl 2-3 x week	☐	☐	☐	☐	☐	☐	☐
Remove uneaten food	☐	☐	☐	☐	☐	☐	☐
Check filter	☐	☐	☐	☐	☐	☐	☐
Check water temperature	☐	☐	☐	☐	☐	☐	☐
Check other equipment	☐	☐	☐	☐	☐	☐	☐
Visual Inspect	☐	☐	☐	☐	☐	☐	☐
	☐	☐	☐	☐	☐	☐	☐

NOTES:

WEEKLY, MONTHLY CHECKLIST

WEEKLY ACTIVITY   DATE: [   ]

- [ ] Test check water quality
- [ ] Change water 20% of the water each week
- [ ] Vacuum up uneaten food and waste
- [ ] Check pH and bacteria levels
- [ ] Healthy checklist

MONTHLY ACTIVITY   MONTH: [   ]

- [ ] Check filters, replacing media as necessary
- [ ] Clean fake plants, decorations, & algae
- [ ] Vacuum up all waste & uneaten food from gravel
- [ ] Check water quality & pH levels

HEALTH CHECKLIST   DATE: [   ]

- [ ] [ ] Fluffy gills
- [ ] [ ] Round belly (same size as head)
- [ ] [ ] Gills back
- [ ] [ ] No skin damage
- [ ] [ ] Active (for an axolotl)

NOTES:

HIGHLIGHT OF THE WEEK:

DAILY CHECKLIST

Activity	WEEK OF						
	SUN	MON	TUE	WED	THU	FRI	SAT
Feed axolotl 2-3 x week	☐	☐	☐	☐	☐	☐	☐
Remove uneaten food	☐	☐	☐	☐	☐	☐	☐
Check filter	☐	☐	☐	☐	☐	☐	☐
Check water temperature	☐	☐	☐	☐	☐	☐	☐
Check other equipment	☐	☐	☐	☐	☐	☐	☐
Visual Inspect	☐	☐	☐	☐	☐	☐	☐
	☐	☐	☐	☐	☐	☐	☐

NOTES:

WEEKLY, MONTHLY CHECKLIST

WEEKLY ACTIVITY   DATE: [ ]

- ☐ Test check water quality
- ☐ Change water 20% of the water each week
- ☐ Vacuum up uneaten food and waste
- ☐ Check pH and bacteria levels
- ☐ Healthy checklist

MONTHLY ACTIVITY   MONTH: [ ]

- ☐ Check filters, replacing media as necessary
- ☐ Clean fake plants, decorations, & algae
- ☐ Vacuum up all waste & uneaten food from gravel
- ☐ Check water quality & pH levels

HEALTH CHECKLIST   DATE: [ ]

- ☐ ☐ Fluffy gills
- ☐ ☐ Round belly (same size as head)
- ☐ ☐ Gills back
- ☐ ☐ No skin damage
- ☐ ☐ Active (for an axolotl)

NOTES:

HIGHLIGHT OF THE WEEK:

DAILY CHECKLIST

Activity	WEEK OF	SUN	MON	TUE	WED	THU	FRI	SAT
Feed axolotl 2-3 x week		☐	☐	☐	☐	☐	☐	☐
Remove uneaten food		☐	☐	☐	☐	☐	☐	☐
Check filter		☐	☐	☐	☐	☐	☐	☐
Check water temperature		☐	☐	☐	☐	☐	☐	☐
Check other equipment		☐	☐	☐	☐	☐	☐	☐
Visual Inspect		☐	☐	☐	☐	☐	☐	☐
		☐	☐	☐	☐	☐	☐	☐

NOTES:

WEEKLY, MONTHLY CHECKLIST

WEEKLY ACTIVITY   DATE: [   ]

- ☐ Test check water quality
- ☐ Change water 20% of the water each week
- ☐ Vacuum up uneaten food and waste
- ☐ Check pH and bacteria levels
- ☐ Healthy checklist

MONTHLY ACTIVITY   MONTH: [   ]

- ☐ Check filters, replacing media as necessary
- ☐ Clean fake plants, decorations, & algae
- ☐ Vacuum up all waste & uneaten food from gravel
- ☐ Check water quality & pH levels

HEALTH CHECKLIST   DATE: [   ]

- ☐ ☐ Fluffy gills
- ☐ ☐ Round belly (same size as head)
- ☐ ☐ Gills back
- ☐ ☐ No skin damage
- ☐ ☐ Active (for an axolotl)

NOTES:

HIGHLIGHT OF THE WEEK:

DAILY CHECKLIST

Activity	WEEK OF						
	SUN	MON	TUE	WED	THU	FRI	SAT
Feed axolotl 2-3 x week	☐	☐	☐	☐	☐	☐	☐
Remove uneaten food	☐	☐	☐	☐	☐	☐	☐
Check filter	☐	☐	☐	☐	☐	☐	☐
Check water temperature	☐	☐	☐	☐	☐	☐	☐
Check other equipment	☐	☐	☐	☐	☐	☐	☐
Visual Inspect	☐	☐	☐	☐	☐	☐	☐
	☐	☐	☐	☐	☐	☐	☐

NOTES:

WEEKLY, MONTHLY CHECKLIST

WEEKLY ACTIVITY   DATE: ☐

- ☐ Test check water quality
- ☐ Change water 20% of the water each week
- ☐ Vacuum up uneaten food and waste
- ☐ Check pH and bacteria levels
- ☐ Healthy checklist

MONTHLY ACTIVITY   MONTH: ☐

- ☐ Check filters, replacing media as necessary
- ☐ Clean fake plants, decorations, & algae
- ☐ Vacuum up all waste & uneaten food from gravel
- ☐ Check water quality & pH levels

HEALTH CHECKLIST   DATE: ☐

- ☐ ☐ Fluffy gills
- ☐ ☐ Round belly (same size as head)
- ☐ ☐ Gills back
- ☐ ☐ No skin damage
- ☐ ☐ Active (for an axolotl)

NOTES:

HIGHLIGHT OF THE WEEK:

DAILY CHECKLIST

Activity	WEEK OF	SUN	MON	TUE	WED	THU	FRI	SAT
Feed axolotl 2-3 x week		☐	☐	☐	☐	☐	☐	☐
Remove uneaten food		☐	☐	☐	☐	☐	☐	☐
Check filter		☐	☐	☐	☐	☐	☐	☐
Check water temperature		☐	☐	☐	☐	☐	☐	☐
Check other equipment		☐	☐	☐	☐	☐	☐	☐
Visual Inspect		☐	☐	☐	☐	☐	☐	☐
		☐	☐	☐	☐	☐	☐	☐

NOTES:

WEEKLY, MONTHLY CHECKLIST

WEEKLY ACTIVITY   DATE: [   ]

- ☐ Test check water quality
- ☐ Change water 20% of the water each week
- ☐ Vacuum up uneaten food and waste
- ☐ Check pH and bacteria levels
- ☐ Healthy checklist

MONTHLY ACTIVITY   MONTH: [   ]

- ☐ Check filters, replacing media as necessary
- ☐ Clean fake plants, decorations, & algae
- ☐ Vacuum up all waste & uneaten food from gravel
- ☐ Check water quality & pH levels

HEALTH CHECKLIST   DATE: [   ]

- ☐ ☐ Fluffy gills
- ☐ ☐ Round belly (same size as head)
- ☐ ☐ Gills back
- ☐ ☐ No skin damage
- ☐ ☐ Active (for an axolotl)

NOTES:

HIGHLIGHT OF THE WEEK:

DAILY CHECKLIST

Activity	WEEK OF	SUN	MON	TUE	WED	THU	FRI	SAT
Feed axolotl 2-3 x week		☐	☐	☐	☐	☐	☐	☐
Remove uneaten food		☐	☐	☐	☐	☐	☐	☐
Check filter		☐	☐	☐	☐	☐	☐	☐
Check water temperature		☐	☐	☐	☐	☐	☐	☐
Check other equipment		☐	☐	☐	☐	☐	☐	☐
Visual Inspect		☐	☐	☐	☐	☐	☐	☐
		☐	☐	☐	☐	☐	☐	☐

NOTES:

WEEKLY, MONTHLY CHECKLIST

WEEKLY ACTIVITY   DATE: [   ]

- ☐ Test check water quality
- ☐ Change water 20% of the water each week
- ☐ Vacuum up uneaten food and waste
- ☐ Check pH and bacteria levels
- ☐ Healthy checklist

MONTHLY ACTIVITY   MONTH: [   ]

- ☐ Check filters, replacing media as necessary
- ☐ Clean fake plants, decorations, & algae
- ☐ Vacuum up all waste & uneaten food from gravel
- ☐ Check water quality & pH levels

HEALTH CHECKLIST   DATE: [   ]

- Y ☐ N ☐ Fluffy gills
- Y ☐ N ☐ Round belly (same size as head)
- Y ☐ N ☐ Gills back
- Y ☐ N ☐ No skin damage
- Y ☐ N ☐ Active (for an axolotl)

NOTES:

HIGHLIGHT OF THE WEEK:

DAILY CHECKLIST

Activity	WEEK OF						
	SUN	MON	TUE	WED	THU	FRI	SAT
Feed axolotl 2-3 x week	☐	☐	☐	☐	☐	☐	☐
Remove uneaten food	☐	☐	☐	☐	☐	☐	☐
Check filter	☐	☐	☐	☐	☐	☐	☐
Check water temperature	☐	☐	☐	☐	☐	☐	☐
Check other equipment	☐	☐	☐	☐	☐	☐	☐
Visual Inspect	☐	☐	☐	☐	☐	☐	☐
	☐	☐	☐	☐	☐	☐	☐

NOTES:

WEEKLY, MONTHLY CHECKLIST

WEEKLY ACTIVITY   DATE:

- [ ] Test check water quality
- [ ] Change water 20% of the water each week
- [ ] Vacuum up uneaten food and waste
- [ ] Check pH and bacteria levels
- [ ] Healthy checklist

MONTHLY ACTIVITY   MONTH:

- [ ] Check filters, replacing media as necessary
- [ ] Clean fake plants, decorations, & algae
- [ ] Vacuum up all waste & uneaten food from gravel
- [ ] Check water quality & pH levels

HEALTH CHECKLIST   DATE:

- [ ] [ ] Fluffy gills
- [ ] [ ] Round belly (same size as head)
- [ ] [ ] Gills back
- [ ] [ ] No skin damage
- [ ] [ ] Active (for an axolotl)

NOTES:

HIGHLIGHT OF THE WEEK:

DAILY CHECKLIST

Activity	WEEK OF						
	SUN	MON	TUE	WED	THU	FRI	SAT
Feed axolotl 2-3 x week	☐	☐	☐	☐	☐	☐	☐
Remove uneaten food	☐	☐	☐	☐	☐	☐	☐
Check filter	☐	☐	☐	☐	☐	☐	☐
Check water temperature	☐	☐	☐	☐	☐	☐	☐
Check other equipment	☐	☐	☐	☐	☐	☐	☐
Visual Inspect	☐	☐	☐	☐	☐	☐	☐
	☐	☐	☐	☐	☐	☐	☐

NOTES:

WEEKLY, MONTHLY CHECKLIST

WEEKLY ACTIVITY   DATE: [   ]

- ☐ Test check water quality
- ☐ Change water 20% of the water each week
- ☐ Vacuum up uneaten food and waste
- ☐ Check pH and bacteria levels
- ☐ Healthy checklist

MONTHLY ACTIVITY   MONTH: [   ]

- ☐ Check filters, replacing media as necessary
- ☐ Clean fake plants, decorations, & algae
- ☐ Vacuum up all waste & uneaten food from gravel
- ☐ Check water quality & pH levels

HEALTH CHECKLIST   DATE: [   ]

- ☐ ☐ Fluffy gills
- ☐ ☐ Round belly (same size as head)
- ☐ ☐ Gills back
- ☐ ☐ No skin damage
- ☐ ☐ Active (for an axolotl)

NOTES:

HIGHLIGHT OF THE WEEK:

DAILY CHECKLIST

Activity	WEEK OF						
	SUN	MON	TUE	WED	THU	FRI	SAT
Feed axolotl 2-3 x week	☐	☐	☐	☐	☐	☐	☐
Remove uneaten food	☐	☐	☐	☐	☐	☐	☐
Check filter	☐	☐	☐	☐	☐	☐	☐
Check water temperature	☐	☐	☐	☐	☐	☐	☐
Check other equipment	☐	☐	☐	☐	☐	☐	☐
Visual Inspect	☐	☐	☐	☐	☐	☐	☐
	☐	☐	☐	☐	☐	☐	☐

NOTES:

WEEKLY, MONTHLY CHECKLIST

WEEKLY ACTIVITY   DATE: [____]

- ☐ Test check water quality
- ☐ Change water 20% of the water each week
- ☐ Vacuum up uneaten food and waste
- ☐ Check pH and bacteria levels
- ☐ Healthy checklist

MONTHLY ACTIVITY   MONTH: [____]

- ☐ Check filters, replacing media as necessary
- ☐ Clean fake plants, decorations, & algae
- ☐ Vacuum up all waste & uneaten food from gravel
- ☐ Check water quality & pH levels

HEALTH CHECKLIST   DATE: [____]

- ☐ ☐ Fluffy gills
- ☐ ☐ Round belly (same size as head)
- ☐ ☐ Gills back
- ☐ ☐ No skin damage
- ☐ ☐ Active (for an axolotl)

NOTES:

HIGHLIGHT OF THE WEEK:

DAILY CHECKLIST

📅 Activity	WEEK OF [ ]						
	SUN	MON	TUE	WED	THU	FRI	SAT
Feed axolotl 2-3 x week	☐	☐	☐	☐	☐	☐	☐
Remove uneaten food	☐	☐	☐	☐	☐	☐	☐
Check filter	☐	☐	☐	☐	☐	☐	☐
Check water temperature	☐	☐	☐	☐	☐	☐	☐
Check other equipment	☐	☐	☐	☐	☐	☐	☐
Visual Inspect	☐	☐	☐	☐	☐	☐	☐
	☐	☐	☐	☐	☐	☐	☐

NOTES:

WEEKLY, MONTHLY CHECKLIST

WEEKLY ACTIVITY   DATE: [   ]

- [ ] Test check water quality
- [ ] Change water 20% of the water each week
- [ ] Vacuum up uneaten food and waste
- [ ] Check pH and bacteria levels
- [ ] Healthy checklist

MONTHLY ACTIVITY   MONTH: [   ]

- [ ] Check filters, replacing media as necessary
- [ ] Clean fake plants, decorations, & algae
- [ ] Vacuum up all waste & uneaten food from gravel
- [ ] Check water quality & pH levels

HEALTH CHECKLIST   DATE: [   ]

- [ ] [ ] Fluffy gills
- [ ] [ ] Round belly (same size as head)
- [ ] [ ] Gills back
- [ ] [ ] No skin damage
- [ ] [ ] Active (for an axolotl)

NOTES:

HIGHLIGHT OF THE WEEK:

DAILY CHECKLIST

Activity	WEEK OF						
	SUN	MON	TUE	WED	THU	FRI	SAT
Feed axolotl 2-3 x week	☐	☐	☐	☐	☐	☐	☐
Remove uneaten food	☐	☐	☐	☐	☐	☐	☐
Check filter	☐	☐	☐	☐	☐	☐	☐
Check water temperature	☐	☐	☐	☐	☐	☐	☐
Check other equipment	☐	☐	☐	☐	☐	☐	☐
Visual Inspect	☐	☐	☐	☐	☐	☐	☐
	☐	☐	☐	☐	☐	☐	☐

NOTES:

WEEKLY, MONTHLY CHECKLIST

WEEKLY ACTIVITY   DATE: [ ]

- [ ] Test check water quality
- [ ] Change water 20% of the water each week
- [ ] Vacuum up uneaten food and waste
- [ ] Check pH and bacteria levels
- [ ] Healthy checklist

MONTHLY ACTIVITY   MONTH: [ ]

- [ ] Check filters, replacing media as necessary
- [ ] Clean fake plants, decorations, & algae
- [ ] Vacuum up all waste & uneaten food from gravel
- [ ] Check water quality & pH levels

HEALTH CHECKLIST   DATE: [ ]

- [ ] [ ] Fluffy gills
- [ ] [ ] Round belly (same size as head)
- [ ] [ ] Gills back
- [ ] [ ] No skin damage
- [ ] [ ] Active (for an axolotl)

NOTES:

HIGHLIGHT OF THE WEEK:

DAILY CHECKLIST

Activity	WEEK OF						
	SUN	MON	TUE	WED	THU	FRI	SAT
Feed axolotl 2-3 x week	☐	☐	☐	☐	☐	☐	☐
Remove uneaten food	☐	☐	☐	☐	☐	☐	☐
Check filter	☐	☐	☐	☐	☐	☐	☐
Check water temperature	☐	☐	☐	☐	☐	☐	☐
Check other equipment	☐	☐	☐	☐	☐	☐	☐
Visual Inspect	☐	☐	☐	☐	☐	☐	☐
	☐	☐	☐	☐	☐	☐	☐

NOTES:

WEEKLY, MONTHLY CHECKLIST

WEEKLY ACTIVITY   DATE: _____

- ☐ Test check water quality
- ☐ Change water 20% of the water each week
- ☐ Vacuum up uneaten food and waste
- ☐ Check pH and bacteria levels
- ☐ Healthy checklist

MONTHLY ACTIVITY   MONTH: _____

- ☐ Check filters, replacing media as necessary
- ☐ Clean fake plants, decorations, & algae
- ☐ Vacuum up all waste & uneaten food from gravel
- ☐ Check water quality & pH levels

HEALTH CHECKLIST   DATE: _____

- ☐ Y ☐ N Fluffy gills
- ☐ Y ☐ N Round belly (same size as head)
- ☐ Y ☐ N Gills back
- ☐ ☐ No skin damage
- ☐ ☐ Active (for an axolotl)

NOTES:

HIGHLIGHT OF THE WEEK:

DAILY CHECKLIST

Activity	WEEK OF						
	SUN	MON	TUE	WED	THU	FRI	SAT
Feed axolotl 2-3 x week	☐	☐	☐	☐	☐	☐	☐
Remove uneaten food	☐	☐	☐	☐	☐	☐	☐
Check filter	☐	☐	☐	☐	☐	☐	☐
Check water temperature	☐	☐	☐	☐	☐	☐	☐
Check other equipment	☐	☐	☐	☐	☐	☐	☐
Visual Inspect	☐	☐	☐	☐	☐	☐	☐
	☐	☐	☐	☐	☐	☐	☐

NOTES:

WEEKLY, MONTHLY CHECKLIST

WEEKLY ACTIVITY   DATE: [   ]

- ☐ Test check water quality
- ☐ Change water 20% of the water each week
- ☐ Vacuum up uneaten food and waste
- ☐ Check pH and bacteria levels
- ☐ Healthy checklist

MONTHLY ACTIVITY   MONTH: [   ]

- ☐ Check filters, replacing media as necessary
- ☐ Clean fake plants, decorations, & algae
- ☐ Vacuum up all waste & uneaten food from gravel
- ☐ Check water quality & pH levels

HEALTH CHECKLIST   DATE: [   ]

- ☐ ☐ Fluffy gills
- ☐ ☐ Round belly (same size as head)
- ☐ ☐ Gills back
- ☐ ☐ No skin damage
- ☐ ☐ Active (for an axolotl)

NOTES:

HIGHLIGHT OF THE WEEK:

DAILY CHECKLIST

Activity	WEEK OF						
	SUN	MON	TUE	WED	THU	FRI	SAT
Feed axolotl 2-3 x week	☐	☐	☐	☐	☐	☐	☐
Remove uneaten food	☐	☐	☐	☐	☐	☐	☐
Check filter	☐	☐	☐	☐	☐	☐	☐
Check water temperature	☐	☐	☐	☐	☐	☐	☐
Check other equipment	☐	☐	☐	☐	☐	☐	☐
Visual Inspect	☐	☐	☐	☐	☐	☐	☐
	☐	☐	☐	☐	☐	☐	☐

NOTES:

WEEKLY, MONTHLY CHECKLIST

WEEKLY ACTIVITY   DATE: [   ]

- [ ] Test check water quality
- [ ] Change water 20% of the water each week
- [ ] Vacuum up uneaten food and waste
- [ ] Check pH and bacteria levels
- [ ] Healthy checklist

MONTHLY ACTIVITY   MONTH: [   ]

- [ ] Check filters, replacing media as necessary
- [ ] Clean fake plants, decorations, & algae
- [ ] Vacuum up all waste & uneaten food from gravel
- [ ] Check water quality & pH levels

HEALTH CHECKLIST   DATE: [   ]

- [Y] [N] Fluffy gills
- [Y] [N] Round belly (same size as head)
- [Y] [N] Gills back
- [Y] [N] No skin damage
- [Y] [N] Active (for an axolotl)

NOTES:

HIGHLIGHT OF THE WEEK:

DAILY CHECKLIST

Activity	WEEK OF	SUN	MON	TUE	WED	THU	FRI	SAT
Feed axolotl 2-3 x week		☐	☐	☐	☐	☐	☐	☐
Remove uneaten food		☐	☐	☐	☐	☐	☐	☐
Check filter		☐	☐	☐	☐	☐	☐	☐
Check water temperature		☐	☐	☐	☐	☐	☐	☐
Check other equipment		☐	☐	☐	☐	☐	☐	☐
Visual Inspect		☐	☐	☐	☐	☐	☐	☐
		☐	☐	☐	☐	☐	☐	☐

NOTES:

WEEKLY, MONTHLY CHECKLIST

WEEKLY ACTIVITY   DATE:

- [ ] Test check water quality
- [ ] Change water 20% of the water each week
- [ ] Vacuum up uneaten food and waste
- [ ] Check pH and bacteria levels
- [ ] Healthy checklist

MONTHLY ACTIVITY   MONTH:

- [ ] Check filters, replacing media as necessary
- [ ] Clean fake plants, decorations, & algae
- [ ] Vacuum up all waste & uneaten food from gravel
- [ ] Check water quality & pH levels

HEALTH CHECKLIST   DATE:

- [Y] [ ] Fluffy gills
- [Y] [ ] Round belly (same size as head)
- [ ] [ ] Gills back
- [Y] [ ] No skin damage
- [Y] [ ] Active (for an axolotl)

NOTES:

HIGHLIGHT OF THE WEEK:

DAILY CHECKLIST

Activity	WEEK OF						
	SUN	MON	TUE	WED	THU	FRI	SAT
Feed axolotl 2-3 x week	☐	☐	☐	☐	☐	☐	☐
Remove uneaten food	☐	☐	☐	☐	☐	☐	☐
Check filter	☐	☐	☐	☐	☐	☐	☐
Check water temperature	☐	☐	☐	☐	☐	☐	☐
Check other equipment	☐	☐	☐	☐	☐	☐	☐
Visual Inspect	☐	☐	☐	☐	☐	☐	☐
	☐	☐	☐	☐	☐	☐	☐

NOTES:

WEEKLY, MONTHLY CHECKLIST

WEEKLY ACTIVITY   DATE: [   ]

- [ ] Test check water quality
- [ ] Change water 20% of the water each week
- [ ] Vacuum up uneaten food and waste
- [ ] Check pH and bacteria levels
- [ ] Healthy checklist

MONTHLY ACTIVITY   MONTH: [   ]

- [ ] Check filters, replacing media as necessary
- [ ] Clean fake plants, decorations, & algae
- [ ] Vacuum up all waste & uneaten food from gravel
- [ ] Check water quality & pH levels

HEALTH CHECKLIST   DATE: [   ]

- [ ] [ ] Fluffy gills
- [ ] [ ] Round belly (same size as head)
- [ ] [ ] Gills back
- [ ] [ ] No skin damage
- [ ] [ ] Active (for an axolotl)

NOTES:

HIGHLIGHT OF THE WEEK:

DAILY CHECKLIST

Activity	WEEK OF	SUN	MON	TUE	WED	THU	FRI	SAT
Feed axolotl 2-3 x week		☐	☐	☐	☐	☐	☐	☐
Remove uneaten food		☐	☐	☐	☐	☐	☐	☐
Check filter		☐	☐	☐	☐	☐	☐	☐
Check water temperature		☐	☐	☐	☐	☐	☐	☐
Check other equipment		☐	☐	☐	☐	☐	☐	☐
Visual Inspect		☐	☐	☐	☐	☐	☐	☐
		☐	☐	☐	☐	☐	☐	☐

NOTES:

WEEKLY, MONTHLY CHECKLIST

WEEKLY ACTIVITY   DATE: [   ]

- [ ] Test check water quality
- [ ] Change water 20% of the water each week
- [ ] Vacuum up uneaten food and waste
- [ ] Check pH and bacteria levels
- [ ] Healthy checklist

MONTHLY ACTIVITY   MONTH: [   ]

- [ ] Check filters, replacing media as necessary
- [ ] Clean fake plants, decorations, & algae
- [ ] Vacuum up all waste & uneaten food from gravel
- [ ] Check water quality & pH levels

HEALTH CHECKLIST   DATE: [   ]

- [ ] [ ] Fluffy gills
- [ ] [ ] Round belly (same size as head)
- [ ] [ ] Gills back
- [ ] [ ] No skin damage
- [ ] [ ] Active (for an axolotl)

NOTES:

HIGHLIGHT OF THE WEEK:

DAILY CHECKLIST

Activity	WEEK OF						
	SUN	MON	TUE	WED	THU	FRI	SAT
Feed axolotl 2-3 x week	☐	☐	☐	☐	☐	☐	☐
Remove uneaten food	☐	☐	☐	☐	☐	☐	☐
Check filter	☐	☐	☐	☐	☐	☐	☐
Check water temperature	☐	☐	☐	☐	☐	☐	☐
Check other equipment	☐	☐	☐	☐	☐	☐	☐
Visual Inspect	☐	☐	☐	☐	☐	☐	☐
	☐	☐	☐	☐	☐	☐	☐

NOTES:

WEEKLY, MONTHLY CHECKLIST

WEEKLY ACTIVITY   DATE: [ ]

- [ ] Test check water quality
- [ ] Change water 20% of the water each week
- [ ] Vacuum up uneaten food and waste
- [ ] Check pH and bacteria levels
- [ ] Healthy checklist

MONTHLY ACTIVITY   MONTH: [ ]

- [ ] Check filters, replacing media as necessary
- [ ] Clean fake plants, decorations, & algae
- [ ] Vacuum up all waste & uneaten food from gravel
- [ ] Check water quality & pH levels

HEALTH CHECKLIST   DATE: [ ]

- [Y] [N] Fluffy gills
- [Y] [N] Round belly (same size as head)
- [Y] [N] Gills back
- [Y] [N] No skin damage
- [Y] [N] Active (for an axolotl)

NOTES:

HIGHLIGHT OF THE WEEK:

DAILY CHECKLIST

📅 Activity

WEEK OF

SUN MON TUE WED THU FRI SAT

Feed axolotl 2-3 x week
☐ ☐ ☐ ☐ ☐ ☐ ☐

Remove uneaten food
☐ ☐ ☐ ☐ ☐ ☐ ☐

Check filter
☐ ☐ ☐ ☐ ☐ ☐ ☐

Check water temperature
☐ ☐ ☐ ☐ ☐ ☐ ☐

Check other equipment
☐ ☐ ☐ ☐ ☐ ☐ ☐

Visual Inspect
☐ ☐ ☐ ☐ ☐ ☐ ☐

☐ ☐ ☐ ☐ ☐ ☐ ☐

NOTES:

WEEKLY, MONTHLY CHECKLIST

WEEKLY ACTIVITY   DATE: [   ]

- ☐ Test check water quality
- ☐ Change water 20% of the water each week
- ☐ Vacuum up uneaten food and waste
- ☐ Check pH and bacteria levels
- ☐ Healthy checklist

MONTHLY ACTIVITY   MONTH: [   ]

- ☐ Check filters, replacing media as necessary
- ☐ Clean fake plants, decorations, & algae
- ☐ Vacuum up all waste & uneaten food from gravel
- ☐ Check water quality & pH levels

HEALTH CHECKLIST   DATE: [   ]

- ☐ ☐ Fluffy gills
- ☐ ☐ Round belly (same size as head)
- ☐ ☐ Gills back
- ☐ ☐ No skin damage
- ☐ ☐ Active (for an axolotl)

NOTES:

HIGHLIGHT OF THE WEEK:

DAILY CHECKLIST

Activity	WEEK OF						
	SUN	MON	TUE	WED	THU	FRI	SAT
Feed axolotl 2-3 x week	☐	☐	☐	☐	☐	☐	☐
Remove uneaten food	☐	☐	☐	☐	☐	☐	☐
Check filter	☐	☐	☐	☐	☐	☐	☐
Check water temperature	☐	☐	☐	☐	☐	☐	☐
Check other equipment	☐	☐	☐	☐	☐	☐	☐
Visual Inspect	☐	☐	☐	☐	☐	☐	☐
	☐	☐	☐	☐	☐	☐	☐

NOTES:

WEEKLY, MONTHLY CHECKLIST

WEEKLY ACTIVITY   DATE: [   ]

- ☐ Test check water quality
- ☐ Change water 20% of the water each week
- ☐ Vacuum up uneaten food and waste
- ☐ Check pH and bacteria levels
- ☐ Healthy checklist

MONTHLY ACTIVITY   MONTH: [   ]

- ☐ Check filters, replacing media as necessary
- ☐ Clean fake plants, decorations, & algae
- ☐ Vacuum up all waste & uneaten food from gravel
- ☐ Check water quality & pH levels

HEALTH CHECKLIST   DATE: [   ]

- ☐ ☐ Fluffy gills
- ☐ ☐ Round belly (same size as head)
- ☐ ☐ Gills back
- ☐ ☐ No skin damage
- ☐ ☐ Active (for an axolotl)

NOTES:

HIGHLIGHT OF THE WEEK:

DAILY CHECKLIST

Activity	WEEK OF	SUN	MON	TUE	WED	THU	FRI	SAT
Feed axolotl 2-3 x week		☐	☐	☐	☐	☐	☐	☐
Remove uneaten food		☐	☐	☐	☐	☐	☐	☐
Check filter		☐	☐	☐	☐	☐	☐	☐
Check water temperature		☐	☐	☐	☐	☐	☐	☐
Check other equipment		☐	☐	☐	☐	☐	☐	☐
Visual Inspect		☐	☐	☐	☐	☐	☐	☐
		☐	☐	☐	☐	☐	☐	☐

NOTES:

WEEKLY, MONTHLY CHECKLIST

WEEKLY ACTIVITY   DATE: [   ]

- ☐ Test check water quality
- ☐ Change water 20% of the water each week
- ☐ Vacuum up uneaten food and waste
- ☐ Check pH and bacteria levels
- ☐ Healthy checklist

MONTHLY ACTIVITY   MONTH: [   ]

- ☐ Check filters, replacing media as necessary
- ☐ Clean fake plants, decorations, & algae
- ☐ Vacuum up all waste & uneaten food from gravel
- ☐ Check water quality & pH levels

HEALTH CHECKLIST   DATE: [   ]

- Y ☐ N ☐ Fluffy gills
- Y ☐ N ☐ Round belly (same size as head)
- Y ☐ N ☐ Gills back
- Y ☐ N ☐ No skin damage
- Y ☐ N ☐ Active (for an axolotl)

NOTES:

HIGHLIGHT OF THE WEEK:

DAILY CHECKLIST

Activity	WEEK OF						
	SUN	MON	TUE	WED	THU	FRI	SAT
Feed axolotl 2-3 x week	☐	☐	☐	☐	☐	☐	☐
Remove uneaten food	☐	☐	☐	☐	☐	☐	☐
Check filter	☐	☐	☐	☐	☐	☐	☐
Check water temperature	☐	☐	☐	☐	☐	☐	☐
Check other equipment	☐	☐	☐	☐	☐	☐	☐
Visual Inspect	☐	☐	☐	☐	☐	☐	☐
	☐	☐	☐	☐	☐	☐	☐

NOTES:

WEEKLY, MONTHLY CHECKLIST

WEEKLY ACTIVITY   DATE: [   ]

- [ ] Test check water quality
- [ ] Change water 20% of the water each week
- [ ] Vacuum up uneaten food and waste
- [ ] Check pH and bacteria levels
- [ ] Healthy checklist

MONTHLY ACTIVITY   MONTH: [   ]

- [ ] Check filters, replacing media as necessary
- [ ] Clean fake plants, decorations, & algae
- [ ] Vacuum up all waste & uneaten food from gravel
- [ ] Check water quality & pH levels

HEALTH CHECKLIST   DATE: [   ]

- [ ] [ ] Fluffy gills
- [ ] [ ] Round belly (same size as head)
- [ ] [ ] Gills back
- [ ] [ ] No skin damage
- [ ] [ ] Active (for an axolotl)

NOTES:

HIGHLIGHT OF THE WEEK:

DAILY CHECKLIST

Activity	SUN	MON	TUE	WED	THU	FRI	SAT
WEEK OF							
Feed axolotl 2-3 x week	☐	☐	☐	☐	☐	☐	☐
Remove uneaten food	☐	☐	☐	☐	☐	☐	☐
Check filter	☐	☐	☐	☐	☐	☐	☐
Check water temperature	☐	☐	☐	☐	☐	☐	☐
Check other equipment	☐	☐	☐	☐	☐	☐	☐
Visual Inspect	☐	☐	☐	☐	☐	☐	☐
	☐	☐	☐	☐	☐	☐	☐

NOTES:

WEEKLY, MONTHLY CHECKLIST

WEEKLY ACTIVITY   DATE: [   ]

- [ ] Test check water quality
- [ ] Change water 20% of the water each week
- [ ] Vacuum up uneaten food and waste
- [ ] Check pH and bacteria levels
- [ ] Healthy checklist

MONTHLY ACTIVITY   MONTH: [   ]

- [ ] Check filters, replacing media as necessary
- [ ] Clean fake plants, decorations, & algae
- [ ] Vacuum up all waste & uneaten food from gravel
- [ ] Check water quality & pH levels

HEALTH CHECKLIST   DATE: [   ]

- [ ] Y [ ] N   Fluffy gills
- [ ] Y [ ] N   Round belly (same size as head)
- [ ] Y [ ] N   Gills back
- [ ] Y [ ] N   No skin damage
- [ ] Y [ ] N   Active (for an axolotl)

NOTES:

HIGHLIGHT OF THE WEEK:

DAILY CHECKLIST

Activity	WEEK OF						
	SUN	MON	TUE	WED	THU	FRI	SAT
Feed axolotl 2-3 x week	☐	☐	☐	☐	☐	☐	☐
Remove uneaten food	☐	☐	☐	☐	☐	☐	☐
Check filter	☐	☐	☐	☐	☐	☐	☐
Check water temperature	☐	☐	☐	☐	☐	☐	☐
Check other equipment	☐	☐	☐	☐	☐	☐	☐
Visual Inspect	☐	☐	☐	☐	☐	☐	☐
	☐	☐	☐	☐	☐	☐	☐

NOTES:

WEEKLY, MONTHLY CHECKLIST

WEEKLY ACTIVITY   DATE: [ ]

- [ ] Test check water quality
- [ ] Change water 20% of the water each week
- [ ] Vacuum up uneaten food and waste
- [ ] Check pH and bacteria levels
- [ ] Healthy checklist

MONTHLY ACTIVITY   MONTH: [ ]

- [ ] Check filters, replacing media as necessary
- [ ] Clean fake plants, decorations, & algae
- [ ] Vacuum up all waste & uneaten food from gravel
- [ ] Check water quality & pH levels

HEALTH CHECKLIST   DATE: [ ]

- [Y] [N] Fluffy gills
- [Y] [N] Round belly (same size as head)
- [Y] [N] Gills back
- [Y] [N] No skin damage
- [Y] [N] Active (for an axolotl)

NOTES:

HIGHLIGHT OF THE WEEK:

DAILY CHECKLIST

Activity	WEEK OF	SUN	MON	TUE	WED	THU	FRI	SAT
Feed axolotl 2-3 x week		☐	☐	☐	☐	☐	☐	☐
Remove uneaten food		☐	☐	☐	☐	☐	☐	☐
Check filter		☐	☐	☐	☐	☐	☐	☐
Check water temperature		☐	☐	☐	☐	☐	☐	☐
Check other equipment		☐	☐	☐	☐	☐	☐	☐
Visual Inspect		☐	☐	☐	☐	☐	☐	☐
		☐	☐	☐	☐	☐	☐	☐

NOTES:

WEEKLY, MONTHLY CHECKLIST

WEEKLY ACTIVITY   DATE: [   ]

- [ ] Test check water quality
- [ ] Change water 20% of the water each week
- [ ] Vacuum up uneaten food and waste
- [ ] Check pH and bacteria levels
- [ ] Healthy checklist

MONTHLY ACTIVITY   MONTH: [   ]

- [ ] Check filters, replacing media as necessary
- [ ] Clean fake plants, decorations, & algae
- [ ] Vacuum up all waste & uneaten food from gravel
- [ ] Check water quality & pH levels

HEALTH CHECKLIST   DATE: [   ]

- [ ] [ ] Fluffy gills
- [ ] [ ] Round belly (same size as head)
- [ ] [ ] Gills back
- [ ] [ ] No skin damage
- [ ] [ ] Active (for an axolotl)

NOTES:

HIGHLIGHT OF THE WEEK:

DAILY CHECKLIST

	Activity	WEEK OF						
		SUN	MON	TUE	WED	THU	FRI	SAT
	Feed axolotl 2-3 x week	☐	☐	☐	☐	☐	☐	☐
	Remove uneaten food	☐	☐	☐	☐	☐	☐	☐
	Check filter	☐	☐	☐	☐	☐	☐	☐
	Check water temperature	☐	☐	☐	☐	☐	☐	☐
	Check other equipment	☐	☐	☐	☐	☐	☐	☐
	Visual Inspect	☐	☐	☐	☐	☐	☐	☐
		☐	☐	☐	☐	☐	☐	☐

NOTES:

WEEKLY, MONTHLY CHECKLIST

WEEKLY ACTIVITY   DATE: [   ]

- [ ] Test check water quality
- [ ] Change water 20% of the water each week
- [ ] Vacuum up uneaten food and waste
- [ ] Check pH and bacteria levels
- [ ] Healthy checklist

MONTHLY ACTIVITY   MONTH: [   ]

- [ ] Check filters, replacing media as necessary
- [ ] Clean fake plants, decorations, & algae
- [ ] Vacuum up all waste & uneaten food from gravel
- [ ] Check water quality & pH levels

HEALTH CHECKLIST   DATE: [   ]

- [ ] [ ] Fluffy gills
- [ ] [ ] Round belly (same size as head)
- [ ] [ ] Gills back
- [ ] [ ] No skin damage
- [ ] [ ] Active (for an axolotl)

NOTES:

HIGHLIGHT OF THE WEEK:

DAILY CHECKLIST

Activity	WEEK OF						
	SUN	MON	TUE	WED	THU	FRI	SAT
Feed axolotl 2-3 x week	☐	☐	☐	☐	☐	☐	☐
Remove uneaten food	☐	☐	☐	☐	☐	☐	☐
Check filter	☐	☐	☐	☐	☐	☐	☐
Check water temperature	☐	☐	☐	☐	☐	☐	☐
Check other equipment	☐	☐	☐	☐	☐	☐	☐
Visual Inspect	☐	☐	☐	☐	☐	☐	☐
	☐	☐	☐	☐	☐	☐	☐

NOTES:

WEEKLY, MONTHLY CHECKLIST

WEEKLY ACTIVITY   DATE: _____

- [ ] Test check water quality
- [ ] Change water 20% of the water each week
- [ ] Vacuum up uneaten food and waste
- [ ] Check pH and bacteria levels
- [ ] Healthy checklist

MONTHLY ACTIVITY   MONTH: _____

- [ ] Check filters, replacing media as necessary
- [ ] Clean fake plants, decorations, & algae
- [ ] Vacuum up all waste & uneaten food from gravel
- [ ] Check water quality & pH levels

HEALTH CHECKLIST   DATE: _____

- [Y] [N] Fluffy gills
- [Y] [N] Round belly (same size as head)
- [Y] [N] Gills back
- [ ] [ ] No skin damage
- [ ] [ ] Active (for an axolotl)

NOTES:

HIGHLIGHT OF THE WEEK:

DAILY CHECKLIST

Activity	WEEK OF						
	SUN	MON	TUE	WED	THU	FRI	SAT
Feed axolotl 2-3 x week	☐	☐	☐	☐	☐	☐	☐
Remove uneaten food	☐	☐	☐	☐	☐	☐	☐
Check filter	☐	☐	☐	☐	☐	☐	☐
Check water temperature	☐	☐	☐	☐	☐	☐	☐
Check other equipment	☐	☐	☐	☐	☐	☐	☐
Visual Inspect	☐	☐	☐	☐	☐	☐	☐
	☐	☐	☐	☐	☐	☐	☐

NOTES:

WEEKLY, MONTHLY CHECKLIST

WEEKLY ACTIVITY   DATE: _____

- ☐ Test check water quality
- ☐ Change water 20% of the water each week
- ☐ Vacuum up uneaten food and waste
- ☐ Check pH and bacteria levels
- ☐ Healthy checklist

MONTHLY ACTIVITY   MONTH: _____

- ☐ Check filters, replacing media as necessary
- ☐ Clean fake plants, decorations, & algae
- ☐ Vacuum up all waste & uneaten food from gravel
- ☐ Check water quality & pH levels

HEALTH CHECKLIST   DATE: _____

- ☐ ☐ Fluffy gills
- ☐ ☐ Round belly (same size as head)
- ☐ ☐ Gills back
- ☐ ☐ No skin damage
- ☐ ☐ Active (for an axolotl)

NOTES:

HIGHLIGHT OF THE WEEK:

DAILY CHECKLIST

Activity	WEEK OF						
	SUN	MON	TUE	WED	THU	FRI	SAT
Feed axolotl 2-3 x week	☐	☐	☐	☐	☐	☐	☐
Remove uneaten food	☐	☐	☐	☐	☐	☐	☐
Check filter	☐	☐	☐	☐	☐	☐	☐
Check water temperature	☐	☐	☐	☐	☐	☐	☐
Check other equipment	☐	☐	☐	☐	☐	☐	☐
Visual Inspect	☐	☐	☐	☐	☐	☐	☐
	☐	☐	☐	☐	☐	☐	☐

NOTES:

WEEKLY, MONTHLY CHECKLIST

- [ ] Test check water quality
- [ ] Change water 20% of the water each week
- [ ] Vacuum up uneaten food and waste
- [ ] Check pH and bacteria levels
- [ ] Healthy checklist

MONTHLY ACTIVITY   MONTH:

- [ ] Check filters, replacing media as necessary
- [ ] Clean fake plants, decorations, & algae
- [ ] Vacuum up all waste & uneaten food from gravel
- [ ] Check water quality & pH levels

HEALTH CHECKLIST   DATE:

- [ ] [ ] Fluffy gills
- [ ] [ ] Round belly (same size as head)
- [ ] [ ] Gills back
- [ ] [ ] No skin damage
- [ ] [ ] Active (for an axolotl)

NOTES:

HIGHLIGHT OF THE WEEK:

DAILY CHECKLIST

Activity	WEEK OF						
	SUN	MON	TUE	WED	THU	FRI	SAT
Feed axolotl 2-3 x week	☐	☐	☐	☐	☐	☐	☐
Remove uneaten food	☐	☐	☐	☐	☐	☐	☐
Check filter	☐	☐	☐	☐	☐	☐	☐
Check water temperature	☐	☐	☐	☐	☐	☐	☐
Check other equipment	☐	☐	☐	☐	☐	☐	☐
Visual Inspect	☐	☐	☐	☐	☐	☐	☐
	☐	☐	☐	☐	☐	☐	☐

NOTES:

WEEKLY, MONTHLY CHECKLIST

WEEKLY ACTIVITY   DATE: [ ]

- [ ] Test check water quality
- [ ] Change water 20% of the water each week
- [ ] Vacuum up uneaten food and waste
- [ ] Check pH and bacteria levels
- [ ] Healthy checklist

MONTHLY ACTIVITY   MONTH: [ ]

- [ ] Check filters, replacing media as necessary
- [ ] Clean fake plants, decorations, & algae
- [ ] Vacuum up all waste & uneaten food from gravel
- [ ] Check water quality & pH levels

HEALTH CHECKLIST   DATE: [ ]

- Y [ ] N [ ] Fluffy gills
- Y [ ] N [ ] Round belly (same size as head)
- Y [ ] N [ ] Gills back
- Y [ ] N [ ] No skin damage
- Y [ ] N [ ] Active (for an axolotl)

NOTES:

HIGHLIGHT OF THE WEEK:

DAILY CHECKLIST

Activity	WEEK OF						
	SUN	MON	TUE	WED	THU	FRI	SAT
Feed axolotl 2-3 x week	☐	☐	☐	☐	☐	☐	☐
Remove uneaten food	☐	☐	☐	☐	☐	☐	☐
Check filter	☐	☐	☐	☐	☐	☐	☐
Check water temperature	☐	☐	☐	☐	☐	☐	☐
Check other equipment	☐	☐	☐	☐	☐	☐	☐
Visual Inspect	☐	☐	☐	☐	☐	☐	☐
	☐	☐	☐	☐	☐	☐	☐

NOTES:

WEEKLY, MONTHLY CHECKLIST

WEEKLY ACTIVITY   DATE: [   ]

- [ ] Test check water quality
- [ ] Change water 20% of the water each week
- [ ] Vacuum up uneaten food and waste
- [ ] Check pH and bacteria levels
- [ ] Healthy checklist

MONTHLY ACTIVITY   MONTH: [   ]

- [ ] Check filters, replacing media as necessary
- [ ] Clean fake plants, decorations, & algae
- [ ] Vacuum up all waste & uneaten food from gravel
- [ ] Check water quality & pH levels

HEALTH CHECKLIST   DATE: [   ]

- [ ] [ ] Fluffy gills
- [ ] [ ] Round belly (same size as head)
- [ ] [ ] Gills back
- [ ] [ ] No skin damage
- [ ] [ ] Active (for an axolotl)

NOTES:

HIGHLIGHT OF THE WEEK:

DAILY CHECKLIST

Activity	WEEK OF 						
	SUN	MON	TUE	WED	THU	FRI	SAT
Feed axolotl 2-3 x week	☐	☐	☐	☐	☐	☐	☐
Remove uneaten food	☐	☐	☐	☐	☐	☐	☐
Check filter	☐	☐	☐	☐	☐	☐	☐
Check water temperature	☐	☐	☐	☐	☐	☐	☐
Check other equipment	☐	☐	☐	☐	☐	☐	☐
Visual Inspect	☐	☐	☐	☐	☐	☐	☐
	☐	☐	☐	☐	☐	☐	☐

NOTES:

WEEKLY, MONTHLY CHECKLIST

WEEKLY ACTIVITY   DATE: [ ]

- [ ] Test check water quality
- [ ] Change water 20% of the water each week
- [ ] Vacuum up uneaten food and waste
- [ ] Check pH and bacteria levels
- [ ] Healthy checklist

MONTHLY ACTIVITY   MONTH: [ ]

- [ ] Check filters, replacing media as necessary
- [ ] Clean fake plants, decorations, & algae
- [ ] Vacuum up all waste & uneaten food from gravel
- [ ] Check water quality & pH levels

HEALTH CHECKLIST   DATE: [ ]

- [ ] [ ] Fluffy gills
- [ ] [ ] Round belly (same size as head)
- [ ] [ ] Gills back
- [ ] [ ] No skin damage
- [ ] [ ] Active (for an axolotl)

NOTES:

HIGHLIGHT OF THE WEEK:

DAILY CHECKLIST

Activity	WEEK OF						
	SUN	MON	TUE	WED	THU	FRI	SAT
Feed axolotl 2-3 x week	☐	☐	☐	☐	☐	☐	☐
Remove uneaten food	☐	☐	☐	☐	☐	☐	☐
Check filter	☐	☐	☐	☐	☐	☐	☐
Check water temperature	☐	☐	☐	☐	☐	☐	☐
Check other equipment	☐	☐	☐	☐	☐	☐	☐
Visual Inspect	☐	☐	☐	☐	☐	☐	☐
	☐	☐	☐	☐	☐	☐	☐

NOTES:

WEEKLY, MONTHLY CHECKLIST

WEEKLY ACTIVITY   DATE: [ ]

- ☐ Test check water quality
- ☐ Change water 20% of the water each week
- ☐ Vacuum up uneaten food and waste
- ☐ Check pH and bacteria levels
- ☐ Healthy checklist

MONTHLY ACTIVITY   MONTH: [ ]

- ☐ Check filters, replacing media as necessary
- ☐ Clean fake plants, decorations, & algae
- ☐ Vacuum up all waste & uneaten food from gravel
- ☐ Check water quality & pH levels

HEALTH CHECKLIST   DATE: [ ]

- ☐Y ☐N   Fluffy gills
- ☐Y ☐N   Round belly (same size as head)
- ☐Y ☐N   Gills back
- ☐Y ☐N   No skin damage
- ☐Y ☐N   Active (for an axolotl)

NOTES:

HIGHLIGHT OF THE WEEK:

DAILY CHECKLIST

Activity	WEEK OF	SUN	MON	TUE	WED	THU	FRI	SAT
Feed axolotl 2-3 x week		☐	☐	☐	☐	☐	☐	☐
Remove uneaten food		☐	☐	☐	☐	☐	☐	☐
Check filter		☐	☐	☐	☐	☐	☐	☐
Check water temperature		☐	☐	☐	☐	☐	☐	☐
Check other equipment		☐	☐	☐	☐	☐	☐	☐
Visual Inspect		☐	☐	☐	☐	☐	☐	☐
		☐	☐	☐	☐	☐	☐	☐

NOTES:

WEEKLY, MONTHLY CHECKLIST

WEEKLY ACTIVITY   DATE: [   ]

- [ ] Test check water quality
- [ ] Change water 20% of the water each week
- [ ] Vacuum up uneaten food and waste
- [ ] Check pH and bacteria levels
- [ ] Healthy checklist

MONTHLY ACTIVITY   MONTH: [   ]

- [ ] Check filters, replacing media as necessary
- [ ] Clean fake plants, decorations, & algae
- [ ] Vacuum up all waste & uneaten food from gravel
- [ ] Check water quality & pH levels

HEALTH CHECKLIST   DATE: [   ]

- [ ] [ ] Fluffy gills
- [ ] [ ] Round belly (same size as head)
- [ ] [ ] Gills back
- [ ] [ ] No skin damage
- [ ] [ ] Active (for an axolotl)

NOTES:

HIGHLIGHT OF THE WEEK:

DAILY CHECKLIST

Activity

WEEK OF

	SUN	MON	TUE	WED	THU	FRI	SAT
Feed axolotl 2-3 x week	☐	☐	☐	☐	☐	☐	☐
Remove uneaten food	☐	☐	☐	☐	☐	☐	☐
Check filter	☐	☐	☐	☐	☐	☐	☐
Check water temperature	☐	☐	☐	☐	☐	☐	☐
Check other equipment	☐	☐	☐	☐	☐	☐	☐
Visual Inspect	☐	☐	☐	☐	☐	☐	☐
	☐	☐	☐	☐	☐	☐	☐

NOTES:

WEEKLY, MONTHLY CHECKLIST

- [ ] Test check water quality
- [ ] Change water 20% of the water each week
- [ ] Vacuum up uneaten food and waste
- [ ] Check pH and bacteria levels
- [ ] Healthy checklist

MONTHLY ACTIVITY   MONTH: [   ]

- [ ] Check filters, replacing media as necessary
- [ ] Clean fake plants, decorations, & algae
- [ ] Vacuum up all waste & uneaten food from gravel
- [ ] Check water quality & pH levels

HEALTH CHECKLIST   DATE: [   ]

- [ ] [ ] Fluffy gills
- [ ] [ ] Round belly (same size as head)
- [ ] [ ] Gills back
- [ ] [ ] No skin damage
- [ ] [ ] Active (for an axolotl)

NOTES:

HIGHLIGHT OF THE WEEK:

DAILY CHECKLIST

Activity	WEEK OF						
	SUN	MON	TUE	WED	THU	FRI	SAT
Feed axolotl 2-3 x week	☐	☐	☐	☐	☐	☐	☐
Remove uneaten food	☐	☐	☐	☐	☐	☐	☐
Check filter	☐	☐	☐	☐	☐	☐	☐
Check water temperature	☐	☐	☐	☐	☐	☐	☐
Check other equipment	☐	☐	☐	☐	☐	☐	☐
Visual Inspect	☐	☐	☐	☐	☐	☐	☐
	☐	☐	☐	☐	☐	☐	☐

NOTES:

WEEKLY, MONTHLY CHECKLIST

WEEKLY ACTIVITY   DATE: [　　　]

- ☐ Test check water quality
- ☐ Change water 20% of the water each week
- ☐ Vacuum up uneaten food and waste
- ☐ Check pH and bacteria levels
- ☐ Healthy checklist

MONTHLY ACTIVITY   MONTH: [　　　]

- ☐ Check filters, replacing media as necessary
- ☐ Clean fake plants, decorations, & algae
- ☐ Vacuum up all waste & uneaten food from gravel
- ☐ Check water quality & pH levels

HEALTH CHECKLIST   DATE: [　　　]

- ☐ Y ☐ N   Fluffy gills
- ☐ Y ☐ N   Round belly (same size as head)
- ☐ Y ☐ N   Gills back
- ☐ Y ☐ N   No skin damage
- ☐ Y ☐ N   Active (for an axolotl)

NOTES:

HIGHLIGHT OF THE WEEK:

DAILY CHECKLIST

Activity	WEEK OF						
	SUN	MON	TUE	WED	THU	FRI	SAT
Feed axolotl 2-3 x week	☐	☐	☐	☐	☐	☐	☐
Remove uneaten food	☐	☐	☐	☐	☐	☐	☐
Check filter	☐	☐	☐	☐	☐	☐	☐
Check water temperature	☐	☐	☐	☐	☐	☐	☐
Check other equipment	☐	☐	☐	☐	☐	☐	☐
Visual Inspect	☐	☐	☐	☐	☐	☐	☐
	☐	☐	☐	☐	☐	☐	☐

NOTES:

WEEKLY, MONTHLY CHECKLIST

WEEKLY ACTIVITY   DATE: ☐

- ☐ Test check water quality
- ☐ Change water 20% of the water each week
- ☐ Vacuum up uneaten food and waste
- ☐ Check pH and bacteria levels
- ☐ Healthy checklist

MONTHLY ACTIVITY   MONTH: ☐

- ☐ Check filters, replacing media as necessary
- ☐ Clean fake plants, decorations, & algae
- ☐ Vacuum up all waste & uneaten food from gravel
- ☐ Check water quality & pH levels

HEALTH CHECKLIST   DATE: ☐

- ☐ ☐ Fluffy gills
- ☐ ☐ Round belly (same size as head)
- ☐ ☐ Gills back
- ☐ ☐ No skin damage
- ☐ ☐ Active (for an axolotl)

NOTES:

HIGHLIGHT OF THE WEEK:

DAILY CHECKLIST

Activity	WEEK OF	SUN	MON	TUE	WED	THU	FRI	SAT
Feed axolotl 2-3 x week		☐	☐	☐	☐	☐	☐	☐
Remove uneaten food		☐	☐	☐	☐	☐	☐	☐
Check filter		☐	☐	☐	☐	☐	☐	☐
Check water temperature		☐	☐	☐	☐	☐	☐	☐
Check other equipment		☐	☐	☐	☐	☐	☐	☐
Visual Inspect		☐	☐	☐	☐	☐	☐	☐
		☐	☐	☐	☐	☐	☐	☐

NOTES:

WEEKLY, MONTHLY CHECKLIST

WEEKLY ACTIVITY   DATE: [   ]

- ☐ Test check water quality
- ☐ Change water 20% of the water each week
- ☐ Vacuum up uneaten food and waste
- ☐ Check pH and bacteria levels
- ☐ Healthy checklist

MONTHLY ACTIVITY   MONTH: [   ]

- ☐ Check filters, replacing media as necessary
- ☐ Clean fake plants, decorations, & algae
- ☐ Vacuum up all waste & uneaten food from gravel
- ☐ Check water quality & pH levels

HEALTH CHECKLIST   DATE: [   ]

- ☐ Y ☐ N Fluffy gills
- ☐ Y ☐ N Round belly (same size as head)
- ☐ ☐ Gills back
- ☐ ☐ No skin damage
- ☐ ☐ Active (for an axolotl)

NOTES:

HIGHLIGHT OF THE WEEK:

DAILY CHECKLIST

Activity	WEEK OF						
	SUN	MON	TUE	WED	THU	FRI	SAT
Feed axolotl 2-3 x week	☐	☐	☐	☐	☐	☐	☐
Remove uneaten food	☐	☐	☐	☐	☐	☐	☐
Check filter	☐	☐	☐	☐	☐	☐	☐
Check water temperature	☐	☐	☐	☐	☐	☐	☐
Check other equipment	☐	☐	☐	☐	☐	☐	☐
Visual Inspect	☐	☐	☐	☐	☐	☐	☐
	☐	☐	☐	☐	☐	☐	☐

NOTES:

WEEKLY, MONTHLY CHECKLIST

WEEKLY ACTIVITY   DATE: [   ]

- [ ] Test check water quality
- [ ] Change water 20% of the water each week
- [ ] Vacuum up uneaten food and waste
- [ ] Check pH and bacteria levels
- [ ] Healthy checklist

MONTHLY ACTIVITY   MONTH: [   ]

- [ ] Check filters, replacing media as necessary
- [ ] Clean fake plants, decorations, & algae
- [ ] Vacuum up all waste & uneaten food from gravel
- [ ] Check water quality & pH levels

HEALTH CHECKLIST   DATE: [   ]

- [Y] [N] Fluffy gills
- [Y] [N] Round belly (same size as head)
- [Y] [N] Gills back
- [Y] [N] No skin damage
- [Y] [N] Active (for an axolotl)

NOTES:

HIGHLIGHT OF THE WEEK:

DAILY CHECKLIST

Activity	WEEK OF						
	SUN	MON	TUE	WED	THU	FRI	SAT
Feed axolotl 2-3 x week	☐	☐	☐	☐	☐	☐	☐
Remove uneaten food	☐	☐	☐	☐	☐	☐	☐
Check filter	☐	☐	☐	☐	☐	☐	☐
Check water temperature	☐	☐	☐	☐	☐	☐	☐
Check other equipment	☐	☐	☐	☐	☐	☐	☐
Visual Inspect	☐	☐	☐	☐	☐	☐	☐
	☐	☐	☐	☐	☐	☐	☐

NOTES:

WEEKLY, MONTHLY CHECKLIST

WEEKLY ACTIVITY   DATE: [ ]

- [ ] Test check water quality
- [ ] Change water 20% of the water each week
- [ ] Vacuum up uneaten food and waste
- [ ] Check pH and bacteria levels
- [ ] Healthy checklist

MONTHLY ACTIVITY   MONTH: [ ]

- [ ] Check filters, replacing media as necessary
- [ ] Clean fake plants, decorations, & algae
- [ ] Vacuum up all waste & uneaten food from gravel
- [ ] Check water quality & pH levels

HEALTH CHECKLIST   DATE: [ ]

- [ ] [ ] Fluffy gills
- [ ] [ ] Round belly (same size as head)
- [ ] [ ] Gills back
- [ ] [ ] No skin damage
- [ ] [ ] Active (for an axolotl)

NOTES:

HIGHLIGHT OF THE WEEK:

MY PET
AXOLOTL LOGBOOK

Printed in Great Britain
by Amazon

17056888R00071